JOCKULARITY

Published by Addax Publishing Group
Copyright © 1998 by Brad Kirkland
Designed by Randy Breeden
Cover Design by Anonymouse Graphics

For Information address:
Addax Publishing Group
8643 Hauser Drive, Suite 235, Lenexa, KS 66215

ISBN: 1-886110-44-1

Distributed to the trade by Andrews McMeel Publishing
4520 Main Street
Kansas City, MO 64111

Library of Congress Cataloging-in-Publication Data

Kirkland, Brad Neil, 1956-
    Jockularity : lower level of thought : the sports cartoons of Brad
Kirkland .
        p.   cm.
    ISBN 1-886110-44-1
    1. Sports–Caricatures and cartoons. 2. American wit and humor,
Pictorial.   I. Title
NC1429.K555A4   1998   98-13672
741.5'973–dc21   CIP

1 3 5 7 9 10 8 6 4 2
Printed in the United States of America

JOCKULARITY
Lower level of thought

MIKE TYSON   DON KING   LEECH   NEANDERTHAL MAN   BOX OF ROCKS

DENTAL Week

LESS ←   → MORE

The Sports Cartoons of Brad Kirkland   Volume 1

ADDAX
PUBLISHING
GROUP

Dedication

I would like to thank the following individuals - without their support this project would have been infinitely more difficult.

Richard Dean, Keith and Susan Durrie, Fred L. Firner, Kevin and Jolene Kreutzer, Linda, Bruce, Emily, and Chris Maclean, Elizabeth and Ralph Studebaker, Carol Upton, the nuts at Callahans and the folks at Saturn. Above all, for my mother, she nagged me all the way - Nancy Jean Firner.

Table of Contents

Introduction

YOU CAN FIND ELVIS BY READING THIS!!

Okay, I'm kidding. Just wanted to make sure you were paying attention to this preface. Lord knows, it would be all too easy for you to just plunge in and start reading all the cartoons and just skip the introduction - betraying yourself for what you are, which is a little better than an animal.

Now, just a word about what you're holding in your hand (I really hope all you're holding is this book.) Recently, while watching yet another late night ESPN event (the history of javelin catching, I believe) I realized sports were becoming very serious business, what with English fans dis-emboweling each other over a soccer game and other nasty acts of die-hard fans.

I took a good look around, I mean a real, good look and discovered there is a serious lack of funny in sports, Bob Uecker not withstanding. So then I decided to do something. I decided to eat a really high fat lunch and take a nap in my office until quitting time. About a month later, it occured to me that we could put out a funny book about sports! Oy Vey!

Now before you blow past this little preface, understand that this book has some regional references peculiar to the Midwest that you may find useful knowing.

The rest of the humor shouldn't be lost on you, the average reader, so you've been forewarned! That's it - you're free to go! Oh, dont forget! Don't take your sports too seriously and always remember to apply to infected area.

LOCAL TOPICS

A few explanations are in order here. First, part of this book is dedicated to the funny aspect of our sports news here in the Midwest, so therefore there may be a few subjects you, the non-Kansas City area resident may not be familiar with. WE DON'T LIKE AL DAVIS. You know, the owner of the Raiders.

There's been a long running feud between our area and ol' rat face and we're slow to forgive and forget around here. Other individuals that won't get the key to our city, are, in no particular order, Steve Bono, Lynn Elliott, George Steinbrenner (jeez, no one likes that guy), John Elway, Al Davis and, of course, Al Davis. Just thought you'd like to know.

Now, the rest of this collection of illustrated guffaws should be pretty simple to understand since a really simple mind drew them. If any cartoon should offend you in any way - tough! Go kick Bobby Knight in the knee, we don't particulary like him either.

CHRISTMAS @ THE BONOS'

14

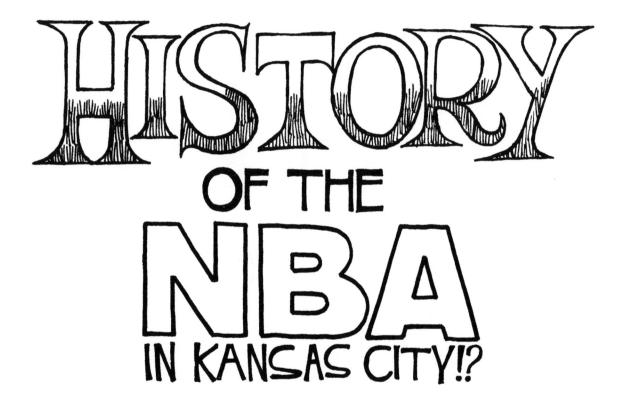

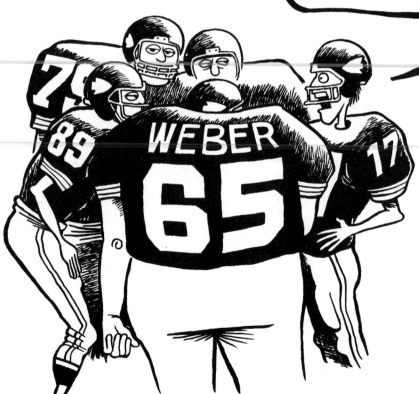

29

INSIDE STEVE BONOŚ MIND

KIRKLAND

33

I'LL TAKE THIS PAGE

KIRKLAND

What the Chiefs do on bye week

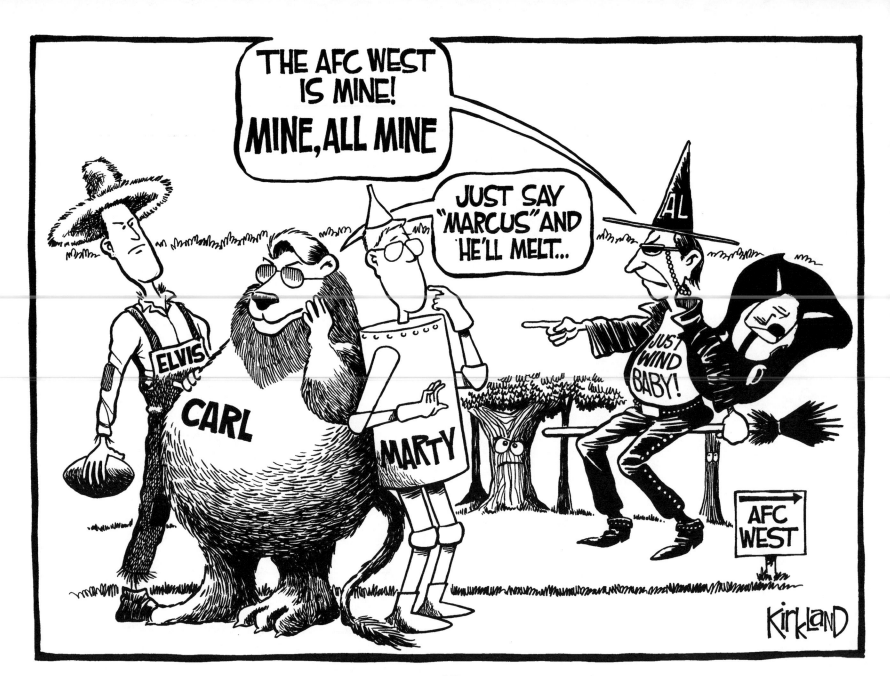

42

44

I TOLD YOU, DON'T STEP IN THE AL DAVIS

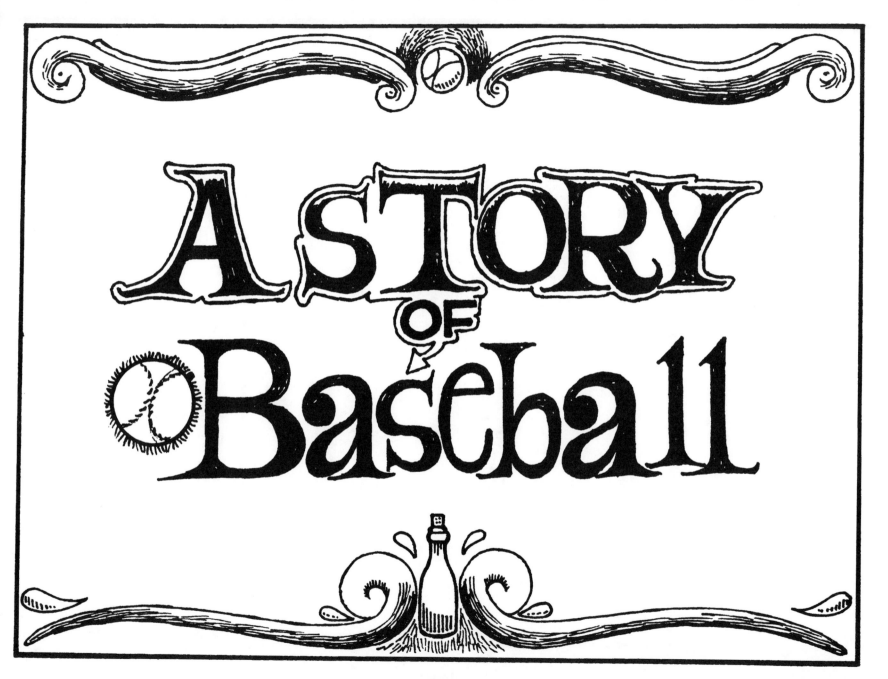

A STORY OF Baseball

A STORY OF BASEBALL

The following story may or may not have occurred, depending on the trust you have in the teller of the tale or your belief in written history. I, for one, think it happened.

In a different time, when baseball was still young, there was a man of much renown, a legend in his age, now swallowed by events of passing history.

A baseball pitcher with no peer he was adored much like current day sports icons – every one knew the name, Mel Famey.

Now Mel so happened to posses a talent that almost equaled that of his pitching prowess. He was the master of the quaff of fine ale, that is to say in layman's terms, he could suck some suds. You know, beer - he drank a lot.

Which brings us to his tale.

Mel played on a team known for it's dearth of talent. They had the swiftest of baserunners, the mightiest of bats, the surest of fielders and, of course, they had the hurler of horsehide's in Mel. They were a juggernaut of a team careening through the summer nights with victory heaped upon victory, seemingly invincible. Oh sure, they had the odd defeat here and there but that was usually due to some lackluster play upon Mel's team behalf not some outstanding play of the opposing team. You get the picture - these guys were good.

Rather than recount the entire season and risk losing your already limited attention, we'll fast forward to the actual occurrence that compelled the telling of this tale (which may or not be true...oh, we already covered that didn't we.) Now bear in mind this all occurred around the turn of the century when social acceptance of some practices were considered normal behavior, such as drinking ale while participating in sport, the idea being that when you played you got hot, so a cool beverage to rejuvenate ones spirit made perfect turn-of-the-century sense. They drank beer on the field while they played. Lots of beer.

Now picture this, O recalcitrant reader, it's a sultry summer night in a town not unlike the one you currently live in (except Cleveland, no one really lives in Cleveland) the air so still

the stadium feels like a tomb and the place is packed beyond capacity. It's the bottom of the ninth in the last game of the World Series with the score tied, bases loaded (and so was Mel), two out and the next batter slowly approaching the plate. Both teams have played to their capacity and drank beyond it also.

The ground around the pitcher's mound is littered with empty bottles of barley pop (beer) as Mel has taken both his talents to new levels never seen before. As the batter takes his spot in the batters box, Mel Famie signals for another beer, perhaps to clear his vision or to further his buzz - history is unclear upon this point. Never-the-less, he takes a slash of the amber ale and hurls on down the pipe. "Ball" screams the ump, who is also awash with the nectar. Two more pitches with the same result have got the hometown crowd in a frenzy. Time stands still as the pitcher collects his thoughts behind the mound and the crowd hushes.

Suddenly, Mel whirls around and stomps to the mound, his face a study of fury and evil intent. He grabs his last bottle of foamy elixir and guzzles it dry in a violent motion, then flings it toward the opposing teams bench almost striking their coach. Through bloodshot eyes most resembling two small, stewed tomatoes, Mel glares at the batter with a look of such unbridled contempt that three people fainted in the first row of seats.

He checked his runners with a sneer and threw his leg high in the air for the wind-up and let free a pitch propelled with all the fury and power that ten men couldn't muster - a fireball that literally seared and scorched the very air that it channeled through, burning its' way through the catchers mitt and embedding itself into the backstop wall with a nasty thud.

"Ball four!" bellows the ump and the crowd erupts with volcano of noise.

Mel hangs his head, spent beyond capacity, as the crowd hoists the other team in victory and carries them off into the velvet night, giddy from the upset and sated with glee.

After the crowd has departed and Mel and his team have reclused themselves deep in the locker room in a cloud of self-pity and despair, two figures remain on the fringes of the field - the winning coach and his assistant. The seasoned veteran of many contests, the coach slowly bends picks up that last bottle of beer hurled at him early and slowly holds it to the diminished light, examining it carefully before delicately folding it into his pocket. "Why would you want that bottle, Coach? It probably still stinks of that insane pitcher of theirs" asked the young assistant. "Because," replied the old man, "it's a piece of history, son. You see, that's the beer that made Mel Famie walk us!"

Okay you've gotten this far, so I think it's safe to assume that you have: **A.** An insane interest in sports.

B. A sincere interest in cartoons. **C.** Absolutely nothing at all to do. This section has more of a general feel, a testament of the sports pulse of the nation, a .... well, cartoons about country-wide stuff. You know, spoiled superstars, temperamental coaches and the ever-popular maniacal fan. If you appreciate a funny look at some issues you've viewed on television or perhaps read in your local sports page, wishing you could have experienced it live, then this is the section you'll want to read again and again. And the book you'll want to purchase again and again so you can look yourself in the mirror and say "I own several copies," with a confidant air.

By the way, if you think, after reading this section that I have a particular dislike of Tyson, you're right! Anybody that can blow $127 million in 6 months has all the business acumen of SPAM and deserves to spend the rest of his life cleaning bird doo out of cuckoo clocks. There I said it. (Sorry about that bird doo part.)

THIS IS YOUR
BRAIN

RODMANS' APPLICATION FOR THE WNBA IS DECLINED...

LET ME GET THIS STRAIGHT-YOU PLAY FOR FUN?!

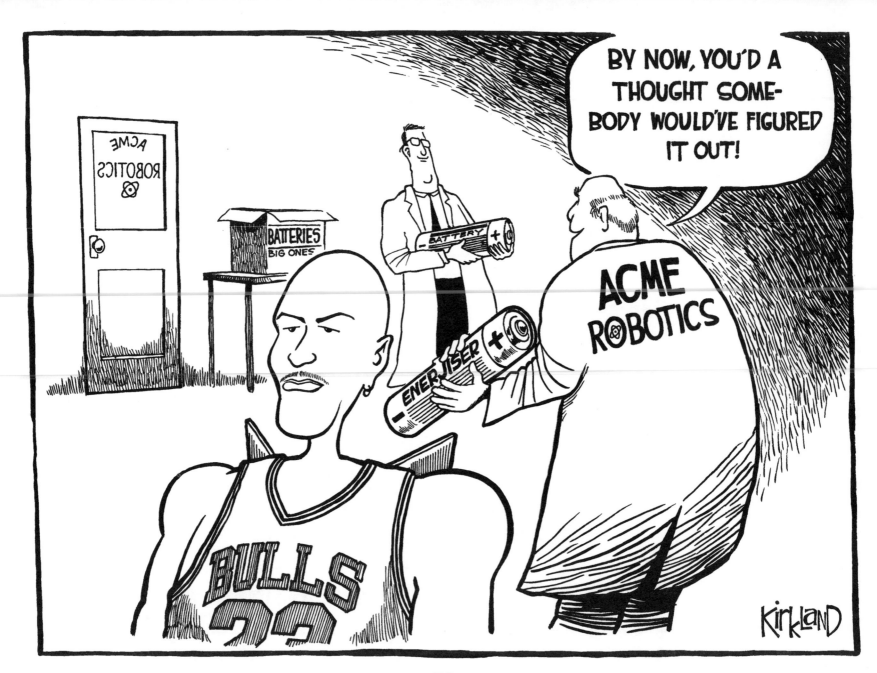

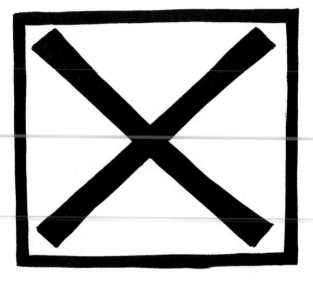

INSIDE MARV ALBERT'S MIND

Hubble Telescope finds Black Hole on Earth!

FUZZY

KIRKLAND

"HIS LEG SEEMS O.K. TO ME"

IN A STRANGE TWIST, THE BALL GETS STUCK IN DICK VITALES' MOUTH

Let's set the record straight right now - I'm not a writer, I'm a cartoonist and yes, there are distinct differences. Normally I draw funny little sports cartoons but just this once I'm going to add some verbage to my cartoons. And the topic of the day is Moundball. And I'm going to explain it to you in detail and probably very poorly.

O.K., so you're sitting in row ZZ in the third inning and the boys of summer have once again whiffed their way through another inning and your attention span has now reached piano recital length. Yet being the die-hard sports nut you are, you feel compelled to stay for the duration. What is going to keep you awake and duly interested? Moundball. Moundball is an oasis of glee in a desert of dull. Moundball is a genuine emerald in the bottom of a stale box of Cracker Jacks (with only two peanuts.) Moundball is skipping Latin class on a warm spring day. Moundball is a diversion from baseball.

Now pay close attention and get that thing out of your mouth! The object of Moundball is very simple – it was designed for fun and monetary gain (two of the most cherished words in America today.) How you play is simple. Have you ever noticed that after every half-inning the baseball is always returned to the mound? You know, after the third out of one team they shift sides and the batting team takes the field. The other fellas that have been sweating like Don King in church come in to take their whiffs at the ball and sit in the dugout, call their agents and scream about a contract extension. Well, in between the running out in the field and the calling of agents, the ball gets returned to the pitchers mound for the next pitcher. Now sometimes it's the catcher who throws it back and sometimes it's one of the umpires and every once-in-a-while it's one of the other players but someone always throws it back to the mound.

Now here's where you and your friends come in. Before each half-inning is over you take a dollar from the buddy of yours seated on the end (the right end, it's tradition.) Take a dollar out of your wallet and pass them to your left until you get to your friend on the end (I'm a poet, don't ya know it.) At this point, the pal on the left end should be holding a buck representing everybody in your little group, including one of his own.

When the half-inning is over all eyes should be glued to the ball because whoever is holding the dough when the ball sticks on the mound gets to keep it! Cool! (Well, it's only cool when you're holding it.) But, hey, you ask, what happens if it doesn't stick? Then what? This is what makes Moundball such a lengthy and profitable game. It never sticks in the dirt! Well, almost never. But after you've ascertained it's rolled off the mound everybody fishes out another dollar and adds it to the pile and passes it down one person. By now you should see a pattern developing here - money in hand, ball doesn't stick, moneys passed down, and so on and so on.

Now the real fun starts after 3 or 4 passes. Fans around you start wondering what all of you are screaming about when not a thing is going on in the game except sweating and calling and running on and off the field. They'll start asking you to explain why you're having such a good time watching a last place team on a 90 degree day in a place where the beer is $25.00 and the bathrooms are slippery. Explain your joy to them and you'll find by the 7th inning stretch every single person in your section will be screaming for that ball to stick on that mound! You'll be the center of attention and the envy of all for discovering a way to enjoy a miserable season of baseball doldrums. Every single one of those fans, tall and small, fat and thin, tattooed and unadorned will love you for it!

That's it. Nothing more. You are now schooled in the proper play and etiquette (there is none) of Moundball. You have the power to defy the boys of summer, of giving you a bummer season and are able to giggle all the way home because of it! All because a cartoonist thought he could write. You lucky dog.

A rivalry usually describes a friendly competition between opposing forces. When applied to the meetings between Kansas University and Missouri University teams, unbridled hate is the closest description available.

To the best of anyones knowledge, the two states seemed to co-exist peacefully for a number of years until the start of our nations' civil war. Given Missouris' pro-slavery stance and Kansas' opposite view, friction was expected. But the solid waste really hit the oscillating appliance in August of 1863.

It was the end of that summer, when a band of Missouri renegades, led by William Quantrell (MU class of '58) burned Lawrence to the ground, killed almost the entire male populace and stole virtually all of the sports equipment in the area. The "rivalry" was born.

Currently, the Kansas Jayhawks/Missouri Tiger rub is the oldest competition west of the Missisippi, second in the nation only to Brown and Dartmouth.

The fever of detest knows no age, gender or status boundaries as evidenced by the remarks of former Missouri governor John Ashcroft. When asked if he'd be inclined to pose in a Jayhawks jersey, he responded by saying "Why don't you go...." well, never mind what he said. To be fair, when former Senator Bob Dole was posed the same inquiry (with an MU shirt), he promptly threw up his spleen. And these are PASSIVE fans!

Nope, no warm and fuzzies here, just complete contempt of those swine on the other side of the border.

What do you call KU fans skydiving?

Skeet.

WHAT DO A ROYALS LEFT FIELDER AND THE MU BASKETBALL TEAM HAVE IN COMMON?

THEY BOTH PLAY "LEFT OUT" IN MARCH...
WELCOME TO THE NCAA TOURNAMENT
MU
KIRKLAND

5. Neighborhood kids trade and collect his teeth

4. Constantly uses phrase "okie dokie"

3. Turned down for a date with Heidi Fleiss

2. Turns you into mall cops for parking in a handicapped spot

1. Tends to sit in the backyard and eat crickets

KIRKLAND

WHAT'S THE DIFFERENCE BETWEEN NORM STEWART & GOD?

GOD DOESN'T THINK HE'S NORM...